Baby Blues® **12** Scrapbook

Lift and Separate

Other Baby Blues® books from Andrews McMeel Publishing

Guess Who Didn't Take a Nap?
I Thought Labor Ended When the Baby Was Born
We Are Experiencing Parental Difficulties. . . Please Stand By
Night of the Living Dad
I Saw Elvis in My Ultrasound
One More and We're Outnumbered!
Check, Please. . .
threats, bribes & videotape
If I'm a Stay-At-Home Mom, Why Am I Always in the Car?

Treasuries

The Super-Absorbent Biodegradable Family-Size Baby Blues®
Baby Blues®: Ten Years and Still in Diapers

Baby Blues® **12** Scrapbook

Lift
and
Separate

by
Rick Kirkman & Jerry Scott

Andrews McMeel
Publishing
Kansas City

Baby Blues is syndicated internationally by King Features Syndicate, Inc. For information, write King Features Syndicate, Inc., 235 East 45th Street, New York, New York 10017.

00 01 02 03 04 BAH 10 9 8 7 6 5 4 3 2 1

ISBN: 0-7407-0455-9

Library of Congress Catalog Card Number: 99-68667

Find *Baby Blues* on the web at
www.babyblues.com

For Sukey . . . and Jan and Paul,
without whom she wouldn't be here.

—R.K.

To Abbey,
who gave me callipidders.

—J.S.

8

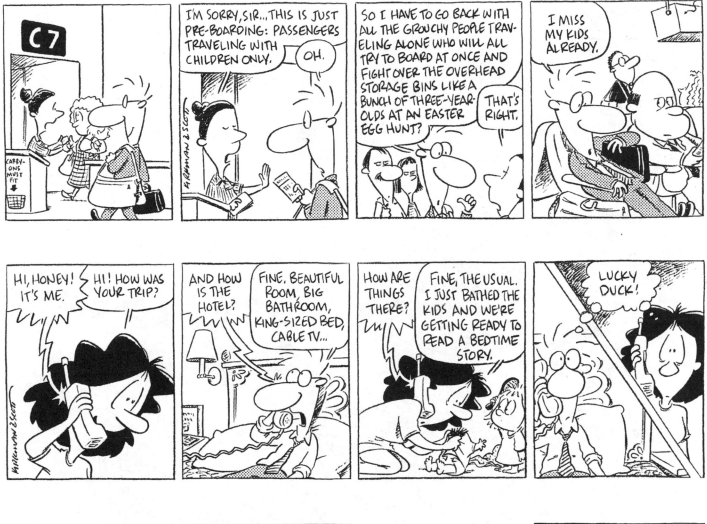

23

Panel 1: MOMMY! DADDY! GRANDPA IS GOING TO HELP US FISH TODAY!

Panel 2: THEN HE SAID WE CAN GO TO THE ZOO, AN' TO THE TOY STORE, AN' THEN WE CAN GO ON THE LAKE 'CAUSE HE BOUGHT US A BRAND-NEW PADDLE BOAT!

Panel 3: YIPPEE!

ippee!

KIRKMAN & SCOTT

Panel 4: KIDS AT A GRANDPARENT'S HOUSE SPOIL FASTER THAN POTATO SALAD IN THE SUN.

CAN WE LIVE HERE FOREVER?

Panel 5: THIS IS GRANDMA'S LITTLE DOG, ZIPPER.

Panel 6: WE HAVE TO BE **VERY** CAREFUL AROUND ZIPPER BECAUSE HE'S NOT USED TO LITTLE KIDS, SO YOU MIGHT UPSET HIM.

Panel 7: SO THAT MEANS NO RUNNING, NO SCREAMING, NO JUMPING AND NO YELLING IN THE HOUSE, OKAY?

OKAY.

TAY.

Panel 8: ZIPPER LOVES KIDS AND YOU KNOW IT!

SHHHHH!

KIRKMAN & SCOTT

Panel 11: WE HAVE TO BE QUIET AROUND ZIPPER, OR ELSE HE GETS UPSET.

Panel 12: I'LL GIVE YOU A HUNDRED BUCKS FOR THE DOG.

KIRKMAN & SCOTT

SIX THINGS YOU DON'T FIND OUT UNTIL YOU'RE A PARENT No. 1

ONE FOUR-YEAR-OLD'S VOICE IS LOUDER THAN 200 ADULT VOICES IN A CROWDED RESTAURANT.

SIX THINGS YOU DON'T FIND OUT UNTIL YOU'RE A PARENT No. 2

A FLUSHING TOILET AND THE WORD "OOPS!" (HEARD TOGETHER) PRODUCE MORE ANXIETY THAN ANY SOUNDS IN NATURE.

SIX THINGS YOU DON'T FIND OUT UNTIL YOU'RE A PARENT No. 3

MEALTIME IS USUALLY ANYTHING *BUT*.

Six things you don't find out until you're a parent

No. 4

The only thing more difficult than not falling asleep while reading a bedtime story is waking up after you have.

Six things you don't find out until you're a parent

No. 5

Blood is thicker than water, but not grape juice.

Six things you don't find out until you're a parent

No. 6

Bribery is not only wrong, it's totally necessary.

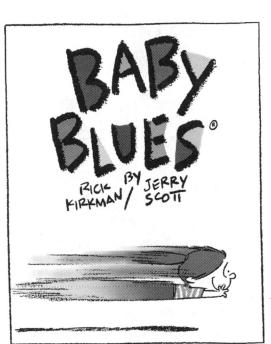

35

Panel 1: SOMETIMES I JUST SIT AND THINK ABOUT WHAT AN INCREDIBLE JOB YOU DO HERE AT HOME WITH THE KIDS.

Panel 2: DAY IN AND DAY OUT... ORGANIZING... EDUCATING... NURTURING... ENTERTAINING...

IT'S MIND-BOGGLING, AND I JUST WANT YOU TO KNOW THAT I APPRECIATE YOU AND ADMIRE YOU.

Panel 4: AN APPROPRIATE RESPONSE WOULD BE, "THANK YOU, HONEY."

YOU HAVE TIME TO "*SIT AND THINK*"???

Panel 5: WHAT ARE YOU DRAWING, ZOE?

IT'S A FLOWER.

Panel 6: I MEAN, IT'S A GIRL. NO, A HORSE. NO, A SWING SET. NO, A BUTTERFLY.

Panel 8: MAYBE I'LL JUST LET YOU KNOW WHAT IT IS WHEN I FINISH IT.

NO RUSH.

KIRKMAN & SCOTT

Panel 1:
≥GASP!≤ ZOE STARTS PRESCHOOL AGAIN IN TWO WEEKS!

THAT CAN'T BE RIGHT.

Panel 2:
LOOK! I WROTE IT ON THE CALENDAR! IT SAYS RIGHT HERE... SEPTEMBER 8TH PRESCHOOL STARTS!

SON OF A GUN.

Panel 4:
IS IT JUST ME, OR DID SUMMERS USED TO LAST LONGER?

I THINK WHEN YOU HAVE KIDS, THEY SHORTEN YOUR CALENDARS.

Panel 5:
WE HAVE TO GO SHOPPING FOR BACK-TO-PRESCHOOL CLOTHES FOR ZOE!

WHAT DO YOU MEAN?

Panel 6:
I **MEAN**, WE HAVE TO GO SHOPPING, WE HAVE TO LET HER PICK SOME THINGS OUT AND TRY THEM ON, AND THEN WE HAVE TO BUY THEM!

Panel 7:
DOES THAT HELP?

NO... I MEANT, WHAT DO YOU MEAN "WE"?

Panel 8:
SAY! HERE'S A THOUGHT!

Panel 9:
I COULD SPEND SOME "GUY TIME" WITH HAMMIE HERE AT HOME WHILE YOU AND ZOE HAVE SOME "GIRL TIME" TOGETHER SHOPPING FOR PRESCHOOL CLOTHES!

Panel 10:

Panel 11:
IN OTHER WORDS, YOU WANT TO BAIL ON ME.

LIKE A RAT FROM A BURNING SHIP.

THIS AFTERNOON ZOE WAS TOTALLY OUT OF CONTROL AND I YELLED AT HER EXACTLY THE WAY MY MOM USED TO YELL AT ME.

AND I MEAN A **BIG** YELL, THE KIND OF YELL THAT STARTS AT YOUR TOES AND COMES ALL THE WAY UP!

IT WASN'T REALLY LIKE ME, YOU SHOULD HAVE SEEN THE LOOK ON ZOE'S FACE. SHE STOPPED DEAD IN HER TRACKS.

HEY, COME ON! DON'T BE ASHAMED...

I'M NOT ASHAMED OF IT... I'M **RECOMMENDING** IT!

BBBBBBBBBB

Z

BBBBBBBBBBBB

BBBBBBBBBBB

YOU STILL LOOK TIRED.

I FEEL LIKE I'VE BEEN RUN OVER BY A TRUCK.

thump! thomp! thud!

NO! NO, HAMMIE!

THAT'S NOT THE WAY WE TREAT MOMMY'S POTS'N'PANS.

YOU HAVE TO USE ONE OF THESE!!

BANG! CLANG! WHANG! BLANG!

THAT WAY, YOU GET MORE ATTENTION.

I'LL TRADE YOU THOSE FOR A COOKIE...

KIRKMAN & SCOTT

62

NOT BAD.

FOR A COUPLE IN THEIR MID-THIRTIES WITH TWO KIDS (TAKING INTO ACCOUNT THAT WE DON'T HAVE TIME TO EXERCISE, THE UNAVOIDABLE GENETIC FACTORS AND THE KNOWLEDGE THAT NEARLY 40% OF AMERICANS ARE OVERWEIGHT)...

...WE LOOK PRETTY GOOD!

YEAH, WHEN YOU PUT IT THAT WAY, I FEEL ALMOST SVELTE!

♪ ROCK-A-BYE BABY IN THE TREE TOP! ♪

♪ HAKUNA MATATA! WHAT A WONDERFUL PHRASE!

♫ WHEN THE WIND BLOWS, THE CRADLE WILL ROCK♪

♪ HAKUNA MATATA! AIN'T NO PASSIN' CRA-A-AZE! ♫

INTERESTING SONG.

THIS WAS EASIER WHEN THERE WAS JUST ONE MUSICAL TASTE TO SATISFY.

THIS PONY'S NAME IS JEWEL HEART FLOWER RAINBOW PRINCESS CANDY CANE ICE CREAM.

OH

AND THIS ONE'S NAME IS GUNKY YUCKY CRYBABY POOPIE BROCCOLI-EATER STINK-A-REENO.

I SEE.

THEY DON'T REALLY GET ALONG TOO WELL.

THAT WOULD HAVE BEEN MY GUESS.

KIRKMAN & SCOTT

65

Panel 1:
WHY IS ZOE TALKING TO HERSELF?
NADINE IS BACK.

Panel 2:
NADINE? ZOE'S INVISIBLE FRIEND?
YES. BUT NOW NADINE IS HER SISTER.

Panel 3:
LOOK AT THAT... SHE'S ACTUALLY PLAYING QUIETLY... NOT FIGHTING WITH HAMMIE... NOT GLUED TO THE TV... AND ALL BECAUSE OF A MAKE-BELIEVE SISTER!

Panel 4:
HONEY, LET'S HAVE MORE INVISIBLE CHILDREN!

Panel 5:
OKAY, ZOE, WHAT BEDTIME STORY DO YOU WANT ME TO READ?
THE PURPLE PUDDING PRINCESS!

Panel 6:
OHHH... NOT AGAIN! I'VE READ THAT EVERY NIGHT THIS WEEK!
PLEASE? I **LOVE** THE PURPLE PUDDING PRINCESS!

Panel 7:
BUT YOU HAVE SO MANY GREAT BOOKS... WHY DO YOU WANT ME TO KEEP READING THIS?

Panel 8:
BECAUSE IT MAKES YOU FALL ASLEEP FASTER THAN MY OTHER ONES.

Panel 9:
SO, HOW WAS YOUR DAY?
WHEW! BUSY!

Panel 10:
I HAD TO DRIVE ZOE TO PRE-SCHOOL, THEN HAMMIE AND I DID THE GROCERY SHOPPING, THEN WE WENT BACK TO PICK UP ZOE. PLUS, THERE WAS THE CLEANING, COOKING AND PLAYING WITH THE KIDS...

Panel 11:
WOW! NO WONDER YOU'RE TIRED!
YEAH.

Panel 12:
YOUR WIFE NEEDS A WIFE.

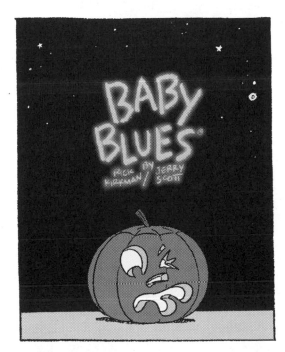

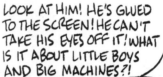

Panel 1: BINK! PLINK! SPLASH! !#& %@!!

Panel 2: I THINK I'M THE LUCKIEST WOMAN IN THE WORLD.

Panel 3: BECAUSE SOMETIMES I FIX STUFF AROUND THE HOUSE?

Panel 4: BECAUSE YOU USUALLY DON'T.

Panel 5: DADDY! LOOK! I WROTE A SEVENTEEN!

Panel 6: NO, SWEETHEART... THAT SAYS "SEVENTY-ONE." SEVENTEEN HAS THE ONE BEFORE THE SEVEN. OH.

Panel 7: FLIP!

KIRKMAN & SCOTT

Panel 8: MOMMY! LOOK! DADDY TAUGHT ME HOW TO MAKE A SEVENTEEN! MAYBE I SHOULD HELP YOU WITH YOUR NUMBERS FROM NOW ON...

Panel 1: TELL ME ABOUT PRESCHOOL TODAY, ZOE.

WELL, FIRST, WE COLORED...

Panel 2: ...THEN BRITTANY MISSED HER MOMMY, SO WE ALL SANG A SONG TOGETHER, BUT MAX DIDN'T SING THE RIGHT WORDS ON PURPOSE, BLAKE WORE ONE ORANGE SOCK AND ONE RED SOCK BY ACCIDENT JUST LIKE NATHAN DID LAST WEEK, AND WILLIAM SMELLED LIKE POPCORN.

Panel 3: TELL DADDY WHAT ELSE HAPPENED.

I GOT IN TROUBLE FOR NOT PAYING ATTENTION.

TO WHAT??

KIRKMAN & SCOTT

Panel 4: LET'S PLAY CATCH, DADDY!

NOT NOW, ZOE... I'M WATCHING THE NEWS SO I KNOW ABOUT ALL THE IMPORTANT STUFF THAT'S GOING ON IN THE WORLD

Panel 5: OH...

Panel 6: IS THERE A LOT OF STUFF MORE IMPORTANT THAN PLAYING CATCH?

Panel 7:

KIRKMAN & SCOTT

Panel 8: 1, 2, 3, 4, 5, 6, 7, 8, 9, 10, 11, 12, 14 ...

Panel 9: ... 16, 18, 20, 22, 23, 26 29, 30, 32, 48, 42, 32, **50**!

Panel 10: SEE? I CAN COUNT!

THAT'S NICE, BUT YOU LEFT OUT A BUNCH OF NUMBERS, SWEETHEART.

Panel 11: I KNOW. I SAVED THOSE FOR YOU.

KIRKMAN & SCOTT

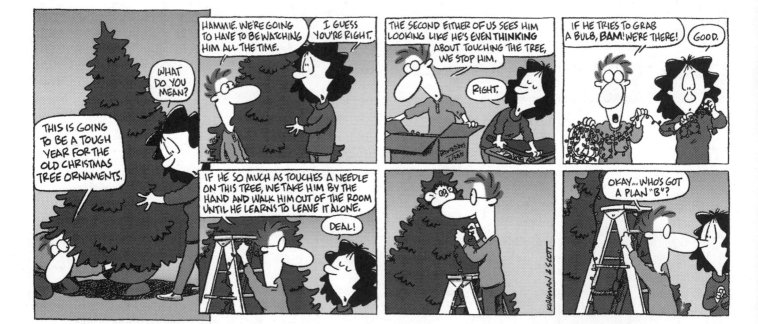

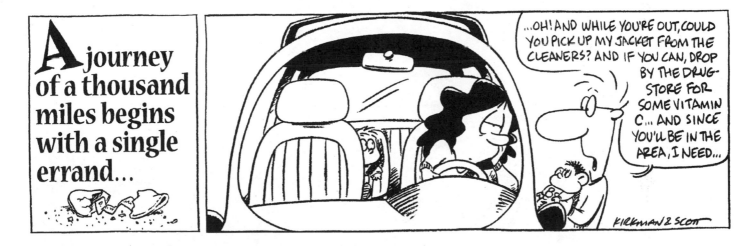

Lesson 1.
If the message is:

"I'd love to hear some insulting comments about my cooking,"

Lesson 2.
If the message is:

"I want you to relax, take your time,"

Lesson 3.
If the message is:

"I'd like a migraine headache, please,"

Lesson 4.
If the message is:

"Please embarrass me in front of the entire grocery store,"

Lesson 5.
If the message is:

"Trash the bathroom,"

Lesson 6.
If the message is:

"Please look at us like we've lost our minds,"

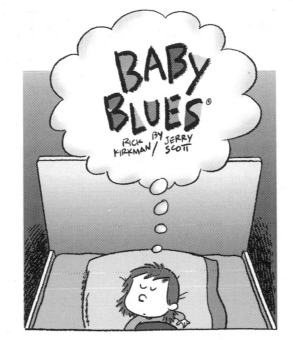

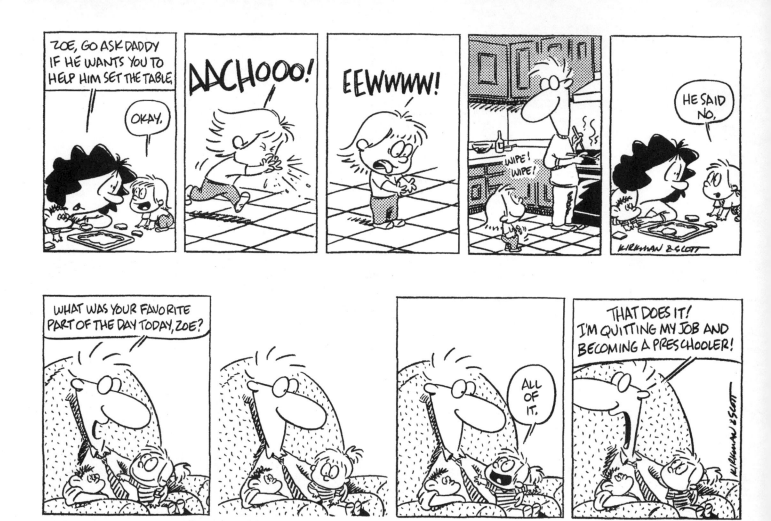

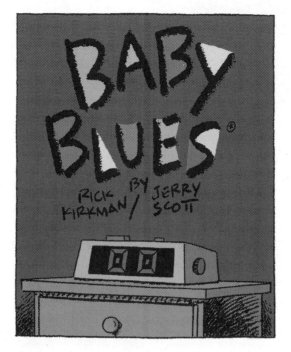

THE VERY BEST THING ABOUT BIRTHDAY PARTIES IS THAT THEY ONLY COME ONCE A YEAR.